365
Meditations
A Spiritual Journey
on the Path of Wisdom

WHITE STAR PUBLISHERS

365
Meditations
A Spiritual Journey
on the Path of Wisdom

CONTENTS

EX

"There is no meditation without wisdom, and there is no wisdom without meditation. When a man has both meditation and wisdom, he is indeed close to Nirvana." The words of prince Siddhartha Gautama, the man who became Buddha, introduce us to the Eastern world that for millennia has had its own vision of reality and existence, made up of endless rivulets flowing from thousands of streams, yet attributable to several identifiable common elements. That which we, in a nutshell, define as "ancient Eastern wisdom", is a vision that tends to look at life from a different perspective, where everything becomes infinitesimal if seen through the eyes of wisdom. The East, the cradle of civilization, was the birthplace of exceptional thinkers and great spiritual masters like Confucius, Lao Tzu and Buddha, whose ideas still influence, permeate and inspire the lives of millions of people today.

Eastern philosophies, often far removed from typical Western rationalism, are characterized by a deep spirituality, where meditation is often indicated as the best way to overcome earthly challenges. Through introspection and seeking serenity and inner peace, people change their view of the world and of their role within it. Ancient teachings from India, China and Japan, from Taoism to Shintoism,

ORIENTE LUX

Zen philosophy and the Chinese I Ching ("Classic of Changes"), speak to us across the centuries and incite us to change the pillars of the traditional beliefs of the West, which is increasingly conditioned and entrapped by the materialistic values of society that dehumanize and impoverish interpersonal relationships. An inner journey, detachment from fears and daily problems, the desire to overcome our physical and psychological limits, with the aim of breaking free from the bonds of circumstances: these are the ways that Eastern wisdom offers those who want to pursue a path of inner discovery. Meditation, concentration and breathing techniques are just some of the tools that the East has given and taught us to help us on our way. It is a path that leads us to overcoming self-consciousness and inner limits, accessible to everyone and simply requiring strong personal motivation. The objective is perhaps difficult to achieve, but we can certainly begin to improve our lifestyle by incorporating a few simple practices into our daily routine.

This volume, full of stunning photos and the thoughts and reflections of eminent figures in Eastern philosophy, is a tribute to the wisdom that the ancient East has offered the world and a stimulus to accompany you on your path to personal growth every day of the year. The evocative images on the following pages will transport you to the most traditional and spiritual part of the East. A place where time stands still; a place that is known for its spirit rather than its geographical features. On your journey through the photographs, you can read the words of the great masters of Eastern wisdom, who will speak to you from the pages with authority, strength and vitality. You will enter into contact with essential truths that will remind you every day that the path to happiness requires awareness, care and profoundness. We need to work on change, on breaking away from desires, on constantly questioning the world and ourselves, on turning our attention to our inner being and personal growth: valuable pieces of wisdom to collect and cherish, to put into practice after you have embraced them. The idea is that when you are leafing through this book, you will be inspired to reflect and find inspiration and an opportunity to relax, thereby enjoying a more harmonious rhythm of life. Finding just a few moments a day to enjoy reading the maxims collected here, will give you the opportunity to take a break from your busy routine and treat yourself to time to reflect on the true essence of life and the core of your problems. Today, meditation is an increasingly common practice, followed by many people seeking well-being in different aspects of their lives. Even scientific research has recently shown that some meditation techniques can help improve concentration and memory in practical activities, as well as being extremely valid tools to control stress and anxiety and to stay healthy. But it is not just about self-reflection: the principles of Eastern wisdom are embodied in many disciplines that are becoming increasingly popular in the West: the concepts of self-control and discipline inherent in various martial arts; the use of the principles of Feng Shui in architecture; the practice of Yoga; the harmony of Ikebana, the Japanese art of flower arrangement; the ancient practice of acupuncture. The voice of the East makes itself heard loud and clear on many occasions, calling us to find a simpler, better and more authentic way to live our lives. This book will help you start your journey on the path to Eastern wisdom.

GIORGIO FERRERO

1

January

They asked: "What is the most important thing to possess?"
"What brings true happiness?"
"What is the most loving act of kindness?"
"What is the best possible way to live?"
Buddha replied:
"Faith is the most important thing to possess."
"Following the path brings true happiness."
"Truth is the most loving act of kindness."
"The practice of introspection is the best possible way to live."

– Buddha

JANUARY

2

January

Three things cannot be long hidden:
the sun, the moon, and the truth.

– Buddha

3

January

A good traveler has no fixed plans
and is not intent on arriving.

– Lao Tzu

4

January

See the false as false,
the true as true.
Look into your heart.
Follow your nature.

– Buddha

5

January

Cut out the love of self,
like an autumn lotus, with your hand!
Cherish the path of peace!

– Buddhist Quote

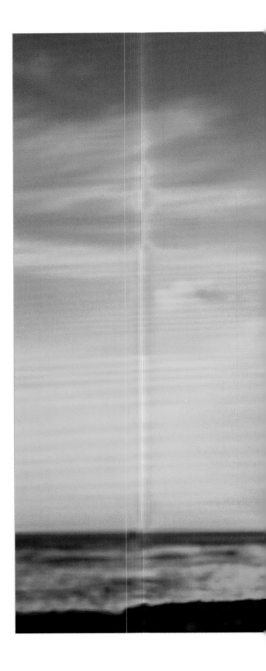

6

January

Where you are right now
is where you are.
You may have a boundless desire to be
somewhere else, doing something else,
but you are not there, you are here.
Live fully in the present moment.

– Zen Proverb

7

January

Salvation must be sought
in the finite itself, there is nothing
infinite apart from finite.

– Daisetsu Teitarō Suzuki

8

January

Although there are many Ways
– the Way of the Gods, the Way
of Poetry, the Way of Confucius – they
all share the clarity of this one mind.

– Takuan Sōhō

9

January

If we would just slow down,
happiness would catch up to us.

– Zen Proverb

10

January

The mind is the root from which all
things grow. If you can understand
the mind, everything else is included.

– Bodhidharma

11

January

Everything is impermanent.
Suffering is a part of existence.
Nothing exists in and of itself.

– Buddhist Quote

12

January

Peace comes from within.
Do not seek it without.

– Buddha

13

January

When I let go of what I am,
I become what I might be.

– Lao Tzu

14

January

With the simplicity of true nature,
there shall be no desire. When there is
no desire, all things are at peace.

– Lao Tzu

15

January

Purity is something
that cannot be attained
except by piling effort upon effort.

– Tsunetomo Yamamoto

16

January

The world is the wise man's monastery;
life is his teacher.

– Zen Proverb

17

January

Zen in its essence is the art of seeing
into the nature of one's own being.

– Daisetsu Teitarō Suzuki

18

January

Keep your hands open,
and all the sands of the desert can pass
through them. Close them,
and all you can feel is a bit of grit.

– Eihei Dōgen

19

January

As a solid rock is not shaken
by the wind,so the wise are not shaken
by blame and praise.

– Buddha

20

January

The journey of a thousand miles
begins with one step.

– Lao Tzu

21

January

Be at peace in the oneness of things,
and all errors will disappear
by themselves.

– Sengcan

22

January

If you forget yourself,
you become the universe.

– Hakuin Ekaku

23

January

A man is not called wise because he talks
and talks again; but if he is peaceful, loving
and fearless then he is in truth called wise.

– Buddhist Quote

24

January

Return to the root
and you will find the meaning.

– Sengcan

25

January

Knowledge is learning something
every day. Wisdom is letting go
of something every day.

– Zen Proverb

26

January

There is no way to happiness.
Happiness is the way.

– Buddha

27

January

Let no one underestimate evil, thinking:
"It will not come near me."
Even a water-pot is filled by the falling of drops of water.
A fool becomes full of evil even if one gathers it little by little.

– Buddha

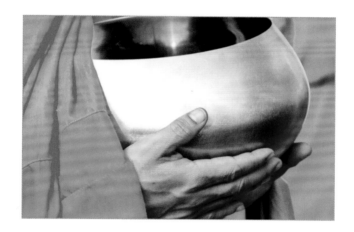

28

January

A seeker asks a Zen teacher: "How can I enter the Way?"
The teacher says: "Do you hear the sound of the mountain stream?"
The seeker says, "Yes, I hear that sound."
And the teacher says, "Enter there."

– Zen Proverb

29

January

The Way is hidden and nameless.
Still only the Way nourishes
and completes.

– Lao Tzu

30

January

Friendship and love
are not asked for like water,
but are offered like tea.

– Zen Proverb

31

January

The opposition between good and evil is often depicted with the struggle between light and darkness, but if we look at it in a different way, we will see that, even when the light shines on darkness, it does not disappear. Instead of being banished, it blends with the light. Becomes light.

– Thich Nhat Hanh

1

February

When you look forward into time,
it seems like forever.
When you look back,
it appears time has passed in a flash.
Start now, from where you are. Use what you have.
Do the best that you can.
What other philosophy of life do you need?

– Zen Proverb

FEBRUARY

2

February

To follow the path look to the master,
follow the master, walk with the master,
see through the master, become the master.

– Sengcan

3

February

The things that happen in our past
remain ours by sharing them with others.

– Lao Tzu

4

February

The teaching is like the raft
that carries you to the other shore.
When you get to the other shore
you must be able to let it go.

– Buddha

5

February

The true Way is sublime. It can't be
expressed in language. Of what use are
scriptures? But someone who sees his
own nature finds the Way, even if he
can't read a word.

– Bodhidharma

6
February

If you walk, just walk.
If you sit, just sit.
But don't wobble.

– Yunmen Wenyan

7
February

Our greatest glory
is not in never falling,
but in rising every time we fall.

– Confucius

8
February

We have to hear the bells
of mindfulness that are sounding all
across our planet. We have to start
learning how to live in a way
that a future will be possible
for our children and our grandchildren.

– *Thich Nhat Hanh*

9
February

The human spirit is as expansive
as the cosmos. This is why it is so tragic
to belittle yourself or to question
your worth.

– *Daisaku Ikeda*

10
February

A Buddha is someone who finds
freedom in good fortune and bad.

– Bodhidharma

11
February

Take the whole universe all at once
and put it on your eyelashes.

– Yunmen Wenyan

12
February

The eye that sees
cannot see itself.

– Zen Proverb

13
February

You are the source of all purity and impurity.
No one purifies another. Never neglect your work for another's,
however great his need. Your work is to discover your work
and then with all your heart to give yourself to it.

– Buddha

14
February

When there is no desire,
all things are at peace.
It is better to light a candle
than to curse the darkness.

– Lao Tzu

15

February

Have the fearless attitude of a hero
and the loving heart of a child.

– Zen Proverb

16

February

Happiness is the absence
of striving for happiness.

– Chuang Tzu

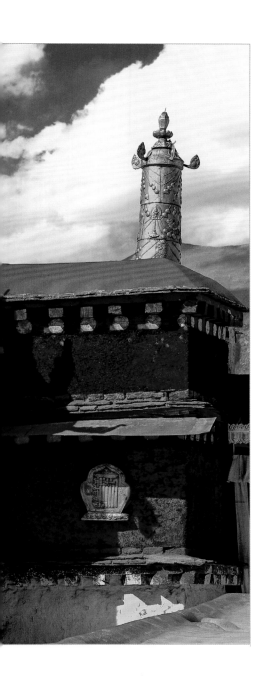

17
February

There are no mundane things outside
of Buddhism, and there is no Buddhism
outside of mundane things.

– *Yuanwu Keqin*

18
February

Our Essence of Mind is intrinsically
pure, and if we knew our mind
and realized what our nature is,
all of us would attain Buddhahood.

– *Huineng*

19

February

What the wise man wants, he seeks within himself. What the common man wants, he seeks within others.

– Confucius

20

February

A superior man is modest in his speech, but exceeds in his actions.

– Confucius

21
February

All know the way,
but few actually walk it.

– Bodhidharma

22
February

Let nature take its course.
By letting each thing act in accordance
with its own nature, everything
that needs to be done gets done.

– Lao Tzu

23

February

Kindness in words creates confidence.
Kindness in thinking creates profoundness.
Kindness in giving creates love.

– Lao Tzu

24

February

When a single flower blooms, the earth arises; when a
single speck of dust appears, the universe is born.

– Zen Proverb

25

February

If you are depressed you are living
in the past. If you are anxious you are
living in the future. If you are at peace
you are living in the present.

– Lao Tzu

26

February

Sometimes your joy is the source
of your smile, but sometimes your smile
can be the source of your joy.

– Thich Nhat Hanh

27

February

Nirvana is right here,
before our eyes.

– Hakuin Ekaku

28/29

February

Be fully aware that everything that has happened
and everything that will happen is in each step you take.
May flowers and fruit always grow
in the places touched by your feet.

– Thich Nhat Hanh

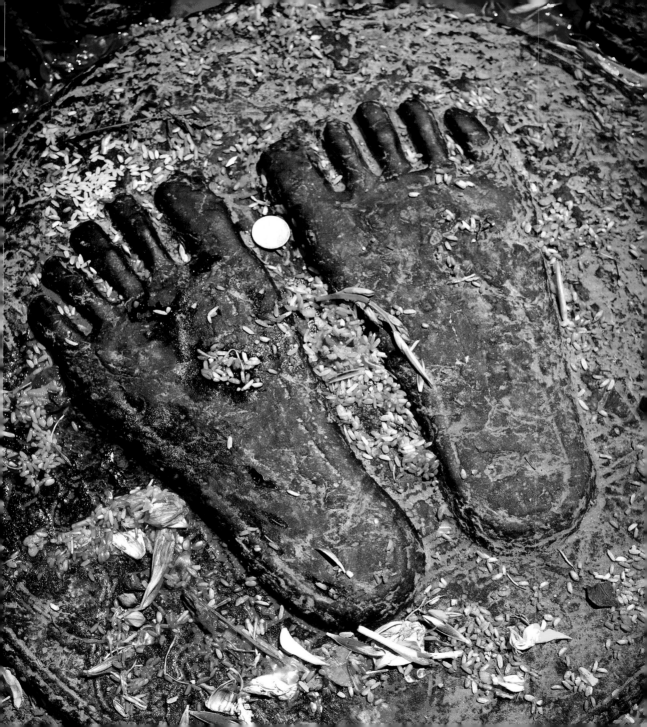

1

March

Enlightenment is like the moon reflected on the water.
The moon does not get wet, nor is the water broken.
Although its light is wide and great, the moon is reflected
even in a puddle an inch wide. The whole moon
and the entire sky are reflected in dewdrops on the grass,
or even in one drop of water.

– Eihei Dōgen

MARCH

2
March

Everybody eats and drinks. But few can distinguish flavors.

– Confucius

3
March

Your true home
is in the here and the now,
it is the door to each single moment.

– Thich Nhat Hanh

4

March

What a strange thing
to be alive beneath cherry blossoms.

– Kobayashi Issa

5

March

See and realize that this world
is not permanent. Neither late
nor early flowers will remain.

– Ryokan Taigu

6
March

When we're deluded there's a world to escape. When we're aware, there's nothing to escape.

– Bodhidharma

7
March

Should you desire great tranquility, prepare to sweat white beads.

– Hakuin Ekaku

8

March

When you get up in the morning, smile at your heart,
at your stomach, at your lungs, at your liver.
After all, much depends upon them.

– Thich Nhat Hanh

9

March

When we are capable of loving ourselves, we are already protecting
and nourishing society. When we are able to smile, to look at ourselves
with compassion, our world begins to change.

– Thich Nhat Hanh

10
March

True wisdom is acquired when we
succeed in understanding ourselves.

– Bodhidharma

11
March

He who knows others is wise;
he who knows himself is enlightened.
He who conquers others is strong;
he who conquers himself is mighty.

– Lao Tzu

12
March

The more you give the richer you become;
the sage holds on to nothing.

– Zen Proverb

13
March

True wisdom is seeing without looking,
hearing without listening.

– Zen Proverb

14

March

Do not shine like jade,
instead be humble like a rock.

– Lao Tzu

15

March

Every day is a good day.
Your every–day mind – that is the Way.

– Yunmen Wenyan

16

March

There are no limits
for those who accept them.

– Zen Proverb

17

March

If the water is still,
the moon is reflected.
If we are still, we reflect the divine.

– Lao Tzu

18

March

Do you have the patience to wait till your mud
settles and the water is clear? Can you remain
unmoving till the right action arises by itself?

– *Lao Tzu*

19

March

Let your spirit move freely
like the wind, never becoming
attached to anything.

– Zen Proverb

20

March

Perhaps you've heard the music
of earth, but you haven't heard
the music of heaven.

– Chuang Tzu

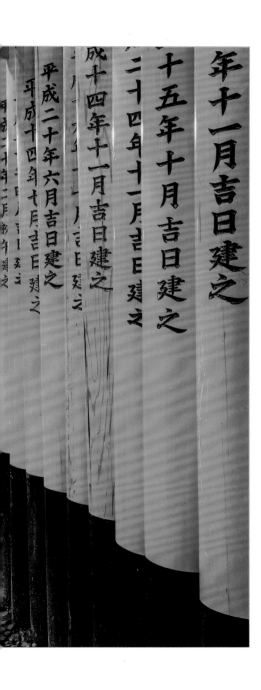

21
March

There are two mistakes one can make
along the road to truth – not going
all the way, and not starting.

– Confucius

22
March

The sage knows himself but makes
no show; he has self–respect
but is not arrogant.

– Lao Tzu

23

March

Difficult problems
are best solved
while they are still easy.

– Lao Tzu

24

March

As long as you're subject
to birth and death,
you'll never attain enlightenment.

– Bodhidharma

25

March

In archery, we have something like the way
of the superior man: when the archer misses
the center of the target, he turns around and
seeks the cause of his failure within himself.

– Confucius

26
March

Only those who have the strength to write
the last word can write the first.

– Lao Tzu

27
March

We are not only responsible for what we do
but also for what we do not do.

– Lao Tzu

28
March

He who has rejected Good and Evil
and practices chastity, working warily in
the world – that one is truly
called a monk.

– Buddhist Quote

29
March

To develop unified understanding
you need to look at alternative
interpretations.

– Eihei Dōgen

30
March

Not knowing how close the Truth is to them, beings seek for it afar. They are like those who, being in the midst of water, cry out for water, feeling thirst.

– Hakuin Ekaku

31
March

Our tendency is to be interested in something that is growing in the garden, not in the bare soil itself. But if you want to have a good harvest, the most important thing is to make the soil rich and cultivate it well.

– Shunryu Suzuki

1

April

Rely on the teachings,
not on the personality of the teacher.
Rely on the meaning of the teachings, not on the words.
Rely on real wisdom,
not superficial interpretation.
Rely on the essence of your pure Wisdom Mind,
not on judgmental perceptions.

– Buddha

APRIL

2

April

Each of us must seek for ourselves,
ask questions for ourselves, understand for ourselves
and awaken for ourselves.

– Zen Proverb

3

April

Keep your purpose in mind with every step you take.
You want freedom. Don't ever forget it.

– Zen Proverb

4
April

Like a fine flower, beautiful to look
at but without scent, fine words are
fruitless in a man who does not act
in accordance with them.

– Buddha

5
April

As a bee gathering nectar does not harm
the color and fragrance of the flower,
so do the wise move through the world.

– Buddha

6
April

Real knowledge is to know
the extent of one's ignorance.

– Confucius

7

April

Practice what you preach.
Before trying to correct others,
do something harder: correct yourself.

– Buddha

8

April

Change is never painful,
only the resistance to change is painful.

– Buddha

9

April

If we don't occupy ourself
with everything, then a peaceful mind
will have nowhere to abide.

– Shenhui

10
April

All beings by nature are Buddhas,
as ice by nature is water.
Apart from water there is no ice;
apart from beings, no Buddhas.

– Hakuin Ekaku

11
April

Stop talking, stop thinking,
and there is nothing
you will not understand. Return
to the root and you will find Meaning.

– Sengcan

12
April

We must find the middle way,
without leaning on one side
or the other, but embracing both.

– Taisen Deshimaru

13
April

If we are peaceful, if we are happy,
we can smile and blossom like a flower,
and everyone in our family, our entire
society, will benefit from our peace.

– Thich Nhat Hanh

14
April

Kindness should become
the natural way of life,
not the exception.

– Buddha

15

April

Ten thousand flowers in spring, the moon in autumn,
a cool breeze in summer, snow in winter.
If your mind isn't clouded by unnecessary things,
this is the best season of your life.

– Sen no Rikyū

16
April

Silence is the greatest revelation.

– Lao Tzu

17
April

Every suffering is a Buddha-seed,
because suffering impels mortals
to seek wisdom.

– Bodhidharma

18
April

Happiness is as light as a feather,
but nobody knows how to bear it.
Calamity is as heavy as the earth,
but nobody knows how to avoid it.

– Lao Tzu

19
April

The mind is always present.
You just don't see it.

– Bodhidharma

20
April

Nothing under heaven is softer or more
yielding than water. Yet for attacking things
solid and resistant, it has no equal. Nothing
can alter water. That the weak can overcome
the strong, and that softness can overcome
the resistant is a fact known by all men.
Yet put into practice by none.

– Lao Tzu

21
April

Never forget:
we walk on hell,
gazing at flowers.

– Kobayashi Issa

22
April

If you have no obstacles
in your own mind, then outer obstacles
will not hinder you or cause you worry.

– Hsuan Hua

23

April

Knowledge is a treasure,
but practice is the key to it.

– Lao Tzu

24

April

Make your mind
as strong as a fortress
and fight temptation with wisdom.

– Buddha

25

April

Waking up this morning, I smile.
Twenty-four brand new hours
are before me.

– Thich Nhat Hanh

26
April

The Way is not in the sky;
the Way is in the heart.

– Buddha

27
April

Care about what other people think
and you will always be their prisoner.

– Lao Tzu

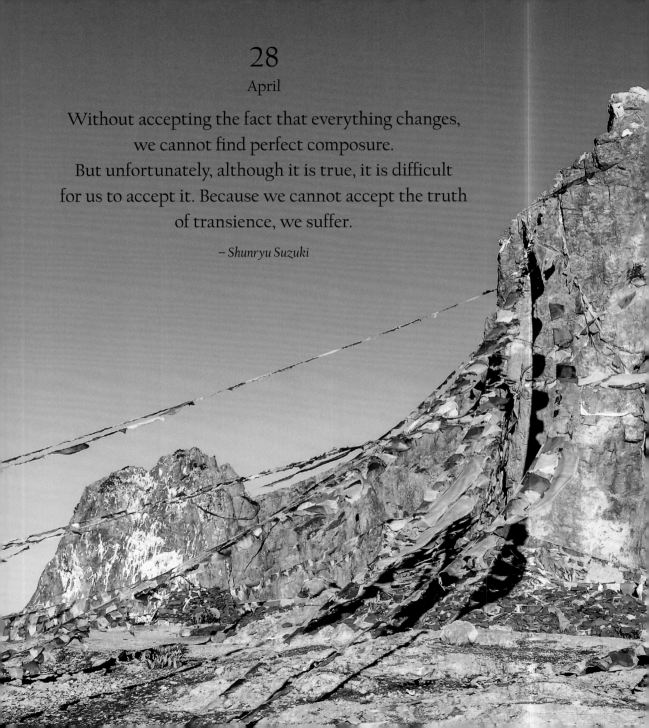

28

April

Without accepting the fact that everything changes,
we cannot find perfect composure.
But unfortunately, although it is true, it is difficult
for us to accept it. Because we cannot accept the truth
of transience, we suffer.

– *Shunryu Suzuki*

29
April

Your body is like a dew-drop
on the morning grass, your life is as
brief as a flash of lightning. Momentary
and vain, it is lost in a moment.

– Eihei Dōgen

30
April

In the beginning the Way is wordless.
It is we that interpret it with words.
But, when you are ready to embrace it,
the words are forgotten.

– Zen Proverb

1

May

Happiness is having friends in a time of need,
happiness is sharing joy,
happiness is knowing you have lived your life
to the full when you die,
happiness is transcending suffering.
Happiness is living virtuously until you are old,
happiness is a solid faith,
happiness is acquiring wisdom,
happiness is avoiding evil.

– Buddha

MAY

2
May

Meditation in the midst of activity
is a thousand times superior
to meditation in stillness.

– Hakuin Ekaku

3
May

Through violence,
you may solve one problem,
but you sow the seeds for another.

– Buddha

4
May

If you cannot find the truth
right where you are, where else
do you expect to find it?

– Eihei Dōgen

5
May

You can't know your real mind
as long as you deceive yourself.

– Bodhidharma

6

May

No one can see their reflection
in running water. It is only in still
water that we can see.

– *Chuang Tzu*

7

May

Happiness is only possible
with true love. True love has the power
to heal and transform the situation
around us and bring
a deep meaning to our lives.

– *Thich Nhat Hanh*

8

May

To attain knowledge,
add things every day. To attain wisdom,
remove things every day.

– Lao Tzu

9

May

Not putting on a display, wise men
shine forth. Not justifying themselves,
they are distinguished. Not boasting,
they achieve recognition. Not bragging,
they never falter.

– Lao Tzu

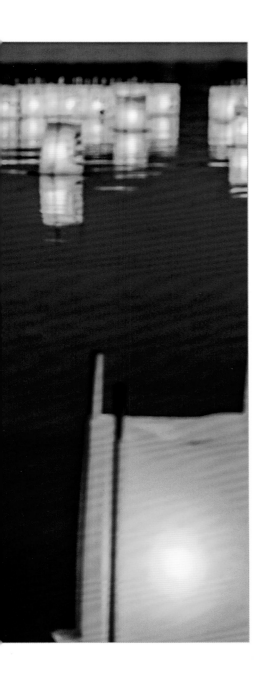

10
May

Those who want to bring light, must first understand the darkness they are about to illuminate.

– Lao Tzu

11
May

If you want to travel the Way of Buddhas and Zen masters, then expect nothing, seek nothing, and grasp nothing.

– Eihei Dōgen

12

May

There is no way to peace; peace is the Way.

– Thich Nhat Hanh

13

May

Seize the moment!
Once it has passed
it can never be lived again.

– Zen Proverb

14

May

A man is not an ascetic (Muni) because
he observes silence (mona), if he is
foolish and ignorant; but the wise who,
taking the balance, chooses the good
and avoids evil, he is a Muni, and is
a Muni thereby; he who in this world
weighs both sides is called a Muni.

– Buddhist Quote

15

May

There is always something to be thankful
for. Don't be so pessimistic if things don't
go the way you want them to.
Always be thankful for the affection
and people that already surround you.
A thankful heart brings happiness.

– Buddha

16
May

To see things in the seed,
that is genius.

– Lao Tzu

17
May

One must be deeply aware
of the impermanence
of the world.

– Eihei Dōgen

18
May

Human life is like a flash of lightning,
transient and illusory, gone in a moment.

– Eihei Dōgen

19
May

Throughout this life, you can never be
certain of living long enough to take
another breath.

– Huangbo Xiyun

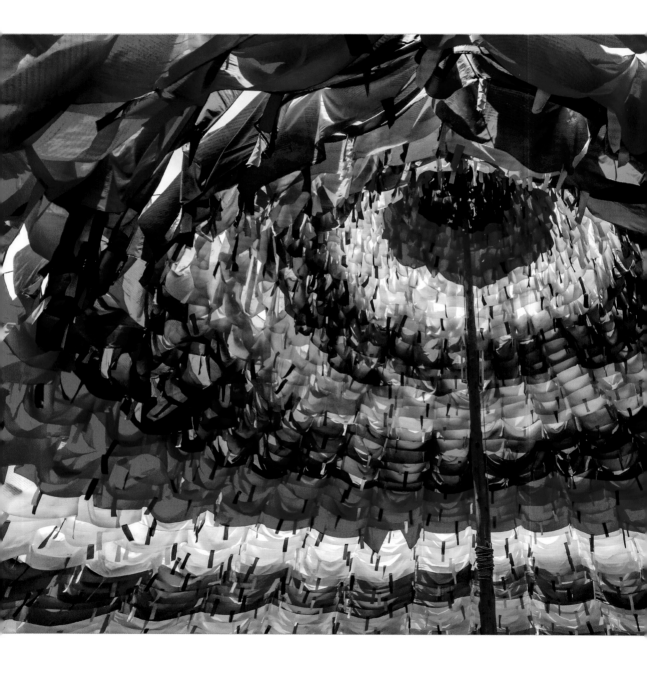

20
May

When silence reaches an ultimate
point, the light penetrates everywhere.

– Hsuan Hua

21
May

Success is as dangerous as failure.
Hope is as hollow as fear.

– Lao Tzu

22
May

Within our impure mind
the pure one is to be found.

– Huineng

23

May

Tomorrow, I will continue to be.
But you will have to be very attentive to see me.
I will be a flower, or a leaf.
I will be in these forms and I will say hello to you.
If you are attentive enough, you will recognize me, and you may greet me.
I will be very happy.

– Thich Nhat Hanh

24

May

Do not regret the past. Look to the future.

– Soyen Shaku

25

May

Many roads lead to the Way,
but basically there are only two:
reason and practice.

– Bodhidharma

26

May

The Great Way is not difficult for those
who have no preferences... If you wish
to see the truth then hold no opinion
for or against. The struggle of what one
likes and what one dislikes
is the disease of the mind.

– Sengcan

27

May

Be a master everywhere and wherever
you stand is your true place.

– Linji Yixuan

28

May

Words have the power
to both destroy and heal.
When words are both true and kind,
they can change our world.

– Buddha

29

May

Those who worship don't know,
and those who know don't worship.

– Bodhidharma

30

May

Do not overrate what you have received,
or envy others. He who envies others
does not obtain peace of mind.

– Buddha

31

May

He who is contented is rich.

– Lao Tzu

1

June

Life is a serious of natural and spontaneous changes.
Don't resist them: that only creates sorrow.
Let reality be reality. Let things flow naturally forward
in whatever way they like.
Rushing into action, you fail.
Trying to grasp things, you lose them.
Forcing a project to completion,
you ruin what was almost ripe.

– Lao Tzu

JUNE

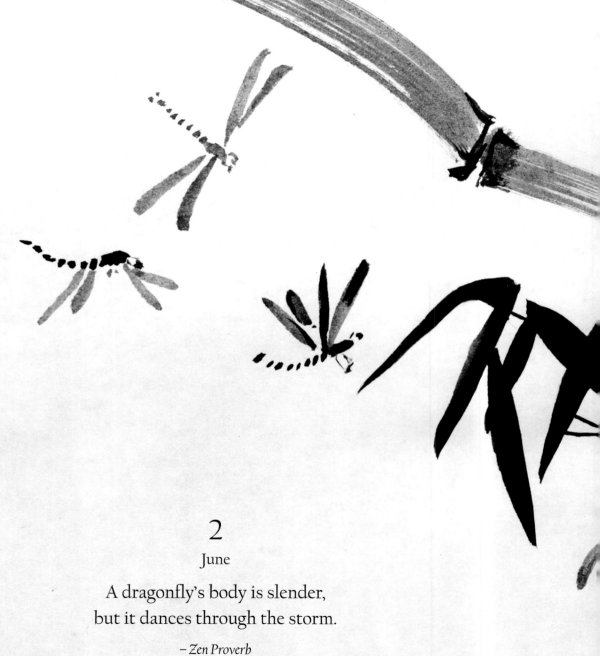

2

June

A dragonfly's body is slender,
but it dances through the storm.

– Zen Proverb

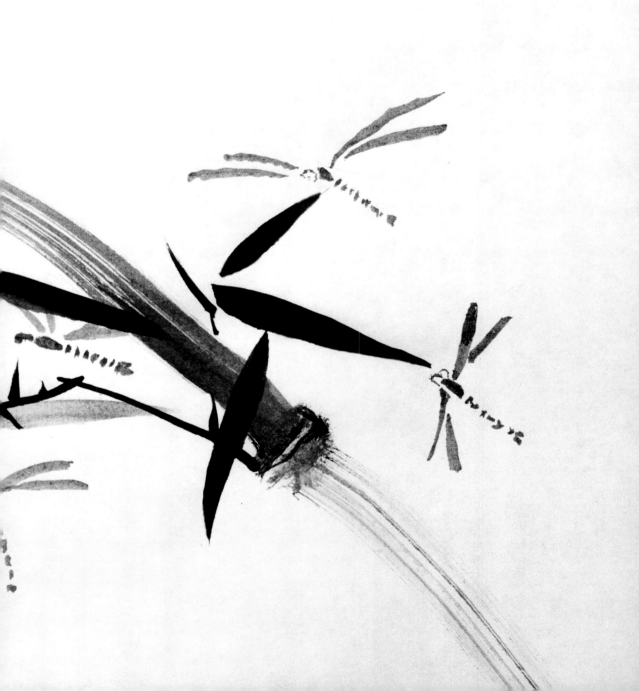

3

June

To study the Buddha Way is to study the self.
To study the self is to forget the self.
To forget the self is to be actualized by myriad things.
When actualized by myriad things, your body and mind
as well as the bodies and minds of others drop away.
No trace of enlightenment remains,
and this no-trace continues endlessly.

– Eihei Dōgen

4

June

If you can't stand ingratitude, think it
over properly before doing any good.

– Confucius

5

June

The most precious gift
we can offer anyone is our attention.

– Thich Nhat Hanh

6

June

A good man does not pretend to be right;
he who pretends to be right is not good.

– Lao Tzu

7

June

My opinion is that you never find happiness
until you stop looking for it.

– Chuang Tzu

8

June

When the entire world recognizes
beauty as beauty, this in itself is ugliness.
When all the world recognizes good as good,
this in itself is evil.

– Lao Tzu

9

June

By three methods
we may learn wisdom:
First, by reflection, which is noblest;
Second, by imitation, which is easiest;
and third by experience,
which is the bitterest.

– Confucius

10

June

Don't chase the past or long for the future. The past has been left behind and the future is not yet here.

– Buddha

11

June

If you use your mind to study reality, you won't
understand either your mind or reality. If you study
reality without using your mind, you'll understand both.

– Bodhidharma

12

June

He who knows his aim feels strong;
this strength makes him calm;
this calmness ensures inner peace;
only inner peace permits deep reflection;
deep reflection is the starting point to every success.

– Lao Tzu

13
June

When you are angry, return to yourself
in order to quell the flames. If someone
makes you suffer, return to yourself
and heal your pain, your fury.

– *Thich Nhat Hanh*

14
June

A Buddha is someone who finds
freedom in good fortune and bad.
Such is his power that karma can't hold
him. No matter what kind of karma,
a Buddha transforms it. Heaven and hell
are nothing to him.

– *Bodhidharma*

15
June

Shape clay into a vessel.
It is the space within that makes it
useful. Therefore profit comes
from what is there, usefulness
from what is not there.

– Lao Tzu

16
June

Because wisdom is innate,
we can all enlighten ourselves.

– Huineng

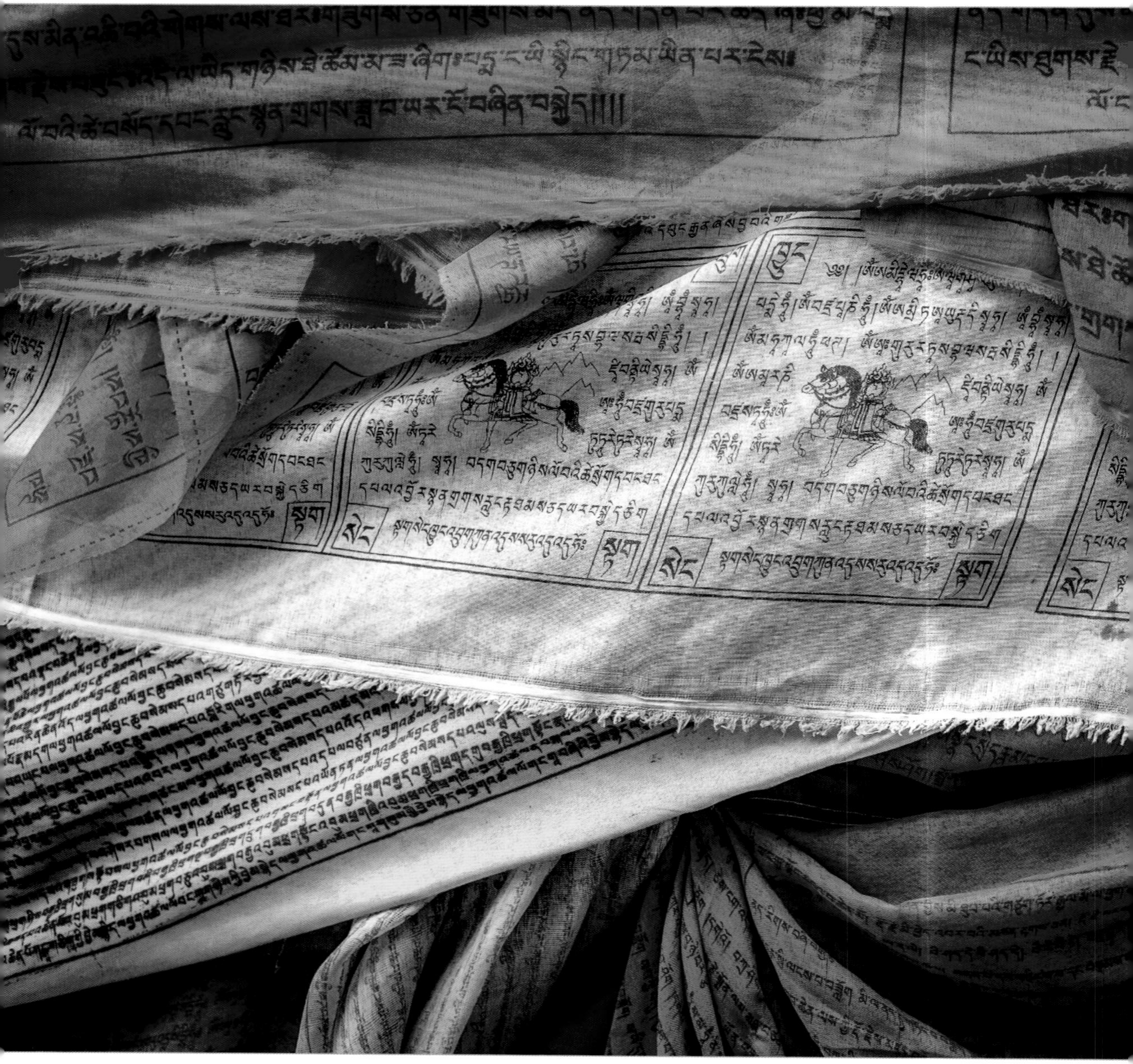

17
June

Truthful words are not beautiful;
beautiful words are not truthful.

– Lao Tzu

18
June

If a person seems wicked, do not cast
him away. Awaken him with your words,
elevate him with your deeds, repay his
injury with your kindness. Do not cast
him away; cast away his wickedness.

– Lao Tzu

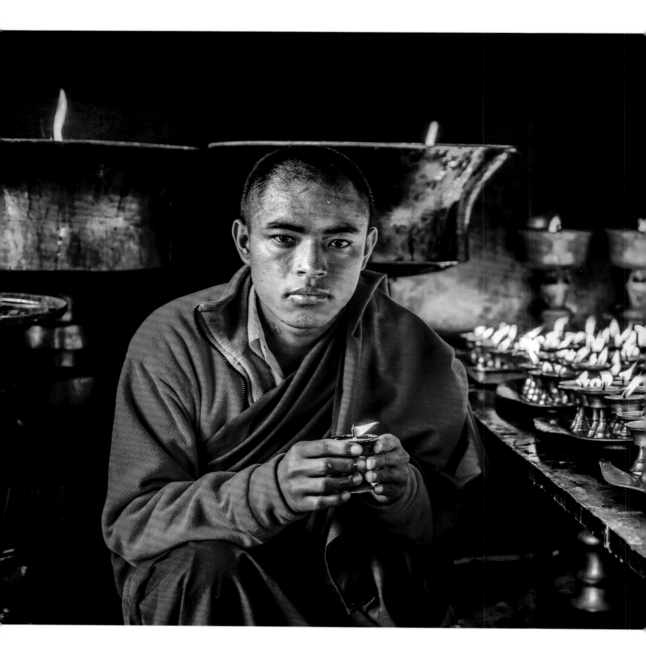

19
June

Which room should you meditate in?
In your heart.

– Eihei Dōgen

20
June

Mastering others requires force;
mastering the self requires strength.

– Lao Tzu

21
June

Flow with whatever may happen, and let your mind be free.
Stay centered by accepting whatever you are doing. This is the ultimate.

– Chuang Tzu

22

June

Have confidence in yourself, not in what you think you should be,
but in who you are.

– *Yoka Daishi*

23
June

If you want to attain enlightenment,
there's no need to study many
teachings. If you adhere to and realize
just one, you will have all the qualities
of a Buddha in the palm of your hand.
Which one? Great compassion.

– Buddha

24
June

You can measure the depth
of a person's awakening
by how they serve others.

– Kōbō Daishi

25
June

To know that you do not know
is the best. To think you know
when you do not is a disease.

– Lao Tzu

26
June

To find perfect composure
in the midst of change is to find Nirvana.

– Shunryu Suzuki

27
June

Our greatest glory
is not in never falling, but in rising
every time we fall.

– Confucius

28
June

Throughout your life advance daily,
becoming more skillful than yesterday,
more skillful than today.
This is never–ending.

– Tsunetomo Yamamoto

29

June

Living mindfully, slowing down
and enjoying each step and each breath,
is enough.

– Thich Nhat Hanh

30

June

To govern you must manifest plainness,
embrace simplicity, reduce selfishness,
have few desires.

– Lao Tzu

1

July

All existing things are really one.
We regard those that are beautiful and rare as valuable,
and those that are ugly as foul and rotten.
The foul and rotten may come to be transformed
into what is rare and valuable,
and the rare and valuable into what is foul and rotten.
Therefore it is said that one vital energy pervades the world.
Consequently, the sage values Oneness.

– Chuang Tzu

JULY

2
July

In the midst of a single breath, where
perversity cannot be held, is the Way.

– Tsunetomo Yamamoto

3
July

Observe things as they are
and don't pay attention to other people.

– Huangbo Xiyun

4

July

If you are not happy here and now,
you never will be.

– Taisen Deshimaru

5

July

If suffering continues, it's because
we keep feeding our suffering.

– Thich Nhat Hanh

6
July

Delusion and the awakening – both can
come and go slowly or suddenly.

– Shenhui

7
July

The foolish reject what they see,
not what they think; the wise reject
what they think, not what they see.

– Huangbo Xiyun

8

July

Just like water doesn't disappear without fire, wisdom doesn't disappear without love. Infinite wisdom and universal love are one with the cosmic order.

– Taisen Deshimaru

9

July

Everything comes from your own heart. This is what one ancient called bringing out the family treasure.

– Yuanwu Keqin

10
July

Being deeply loved by someone gives
you strength, while loving someone
deeply gives you courage.

– Lao Tzu

11

July

In the battle between the river
and the rock, the river will always win.
Not through strength but by persistence.

– Buddha

12

July

If you tell me, I will listen.
If you show me, I will see.
But if you let me experience, I will learn.

– Lao Tzu

13

July

The purpose is not the purpose, it is the Way.

– Lao Tzu

14
July

You must concentrate upon
and consecrate yourself wholly
to each day, as though a fire
were raging in your hair.

– Taisen Deshimaru

15
July

The essence of the Way is detachment.
And the goal of those who practice
is freedom from appearances.

– Bodhidharma

16

July

If we could see the miracle of a single
flower clearly, our whole life would
change.

– *Buddha*

17

July

If one abandons all vain disputation one
will arrive at the position that dharmas
originally neither arise nor perish.

– *Dengyō Daishi*

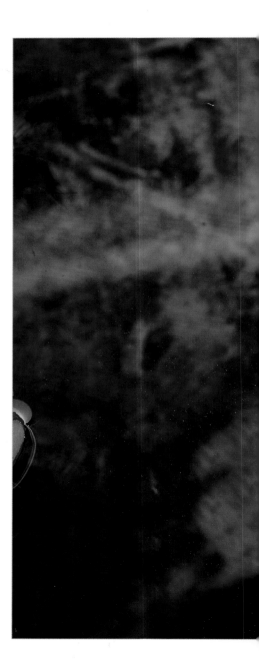

18
July

We are shaped by our thoughts;
we become what we think.
When the mind is pure, joy follows
like a shadow that never leaves.

– Buddha

19
July

Calm and balance are essential
elements in all things; it is important
to break the rhythm every now
and again. If we increase our vitality,
we refresh our mind. You cannot create
any value if you work yourself
into the ground.

– Daisaku Ikeda

20

July

Do not follow in the footsteps
of the wise; seek what they sought.

– *Matsuo Bashō*

21

July

At the bottom of great doubt lies
great awakening. If you doubt fully,
you will awaken fully.

– *Hakuin Ekaku*

22

July

Good words shall gain you honor
in the marketplace, but good deeds
shall gain you friends among men.

– Lao Tzu

23

July

There is no illusion
greater than fear.

– Lao Tzu

24

July

Be your own light.

– Buddha

25

July

Do not turn your mind
into a battlefield, do not have a war
there, for all of your feelings – joy, pain,
anger, hate – are part of yourself.

– Thich Nhat Hanh

26

July

The superior person uses his mind like
a mirror: it accepts all, it reflects all.
It receives, but it does not keep.

– Chuang Tzu

27

July

He who doesn't trust enough
will not be trusted.

– Lao Tzu

28

July

By amending our mistakes, we get wisdom.
By defending our faults, we betray an unsound mind.

– *Huineng*

29

July

I live in a very small house, but my windows
look out on a very large world.

– *Confucius*

30
July

People are scared to empty their minds,
fearing that they will be engulfed
by the void. What they don't realize
is that their own mind is the void.

– Huangbo Xiyun

31
July

If you want to realize the truth,
don't be for or against. The struggle
between good and evil is the primal
disease of the mind.

– Sengcan

1

August

The highest good is like water.
Water gives life to the ten thousand things and does not strive.
It flows in places men reject and so is like the Tao.
In dwelling, be close to the land.
In meditation, go deep in the heart.
In dealing with others, be gentle and kind.
In speech, be true. In ruling, be just.
In business, be competent.
In action, watch the timing.
No fight. No blame.

– Lao Tzu

AUGUST

2
August

The real secret of the arts is to always
be a beginner. In the beginner's mind
there are many possibilities,
but in the expert's there are few.

– Shunryu Suzuki

3
August

Why do you so earnestly seek
the truth in distant places?
Look for delusion and truth
in the bottom of your own heart.

– Ryokan Taigu

4

August

Silence is a true friend
who never betrays.

– Confucius

5

August

When you breathe in, you come back to your body.
When you breathe out, you release all the tension.

– Thich Nhat Hanh

6

August

When the flower blooms, fragrance
spreads. When you attain to your
innermost being, love spreads.
Love is the fragrance.

– Osho

7

August

But while success and failure
depend on conditions,
the mind neither waxes nor wanes.

– Bodhidharma

8

August

The Buddha nature is inside you,
throughout your body, in every cell.

– Taisen Deshimaru

9

August

Do your work, then step back.
The only path to serenity.

– Lao Tzu

10

August

Great intelligence embraces.
Little intelligence discriminates.

– Chuang Tzu

11

August

Some lose yet gain,
others gain and yet lose.

– Lao Tzu

12

August

Perfection is the willingness
to be imperfect.

– Lao Tzu

13

August

Recognizing our emotions without
judging them or pushing them away,
consciously embracing them,
means going back to yourself.

– Thich Nhat Hanh

14

August

He who knows that enough is enough
will always have enough.

– Lao Tzu

15

August

Knowing others is intelligence;
knowing yourself is true wisdom.

– Lao Tzu

16

August

He who stands on tiptoe is not steady.

– Lao Tzu

17
August

Winners find a way,
losers find an excuse.

– Lao Tzu

18
August

A falling tree makes more noise
than a growing forest.

– Lao Tzu

19

August

Keep your heart clear and transparent,
and you will never be bound.
A single disturbed thought
creates ten thousand distractions.

– *Ryokan Taigu*

20

August

To enter the Buddha Way is to stop
discriminating between good and evil
and to cast aside the mind that says
this is good and that is bad.

– *Eihei Dōgen*

21

August

Do you imagine the universe is agitated?
Go into the desert at night and look
at the stars. This practice should
answer the question.

– Lao Tzu

22

August

As a poorly covered house is penetrated
by rain, thus an undeveloped mind
is penetrated by passion.

– Buddha

23
August

It all depends on the character of the people. The decisions of human beings determine not only their fate, but also that of the rest of the world.

– Daisaku Ikeda

24
August

The Way of the sage is to act but not to compete.

– Lao Tzu

25

August

He who saves will suffer heavy loss.
A contented man is never disappointed.
He who knows when to stop
does not find himself in trouble.
He will stay forever safe.

– Lao Tzu

26

August

If you have a problem that can be fixed,
then there is no use in worrying.
If you have a problem that cannot be
fixed, then there is no use in worrying.

– Lao Tzu

27
August

You have to do your own work;
those who have attained enlightenment
can only show you the way.

– Buddha

28
August

Not thinking about anything is Zen.
Once you know this, walking,
sitting, or lying down,
everything you do is Zen.

– Bodhidharma

29
August

Do not seek to follow in the footsteps
of the men of old; seek what they sought.

– Kōbō Daishi

30
August

The sage does not boast of himself,
but does what he must do.

– Zen Proverb

31

August

To lead people walk behind them.

– *Lao Tzu*

1

September

Our way of walking on the Earth has a great influence on animals
and plants. Yet we act as if our daily lives have nothing to do
with the condition of the world. We are like sleepwalkers,
not knowing what we are doing or where we are heading. The future
of all life, including our own, depends on our mindful steps.
We have to hear the bells of mindfulness that are sounding all across
our planet. We have to start learning how to live in a way so that
a future will be possible for our children and our grandchildren.
Our own life has to be our message.

– Thich Nhat Hanh

SEPTEMBER

2

September

The superior man accords with the course of the Mean. Though he may be all unknown, unregarded by the world, he feels no regret — It is only the sage who is able for this.

– Confucius

3

September

A good man does not argue;
he who argues is not a good man.

– Lao Tzu

4

September

Where you stand, where you are,
that's what your life is right there,
regardless of how painful it is or how
enjoyable it is. That's what it is.

– Taizan Maezumi

5

September

A tree as big as a man's embrace springs
from a tiny sprout.
A tower nine stories high begins
with a heap of earth.

– Lao Tzu

6

September

If you try to grasp Zen in movement, it goes into
stillness. If you try to grasp Zen in stillness, it goes
into movement. It is like a fish hidden in a spring,
drumming up waves and dancing independently.

– *Linji Yixuan*

7

September

The Master observes the world
but trusts his inner vision.

– Lao Tzu

8

September

The sage stays behind, thus he is ahead.
He is detached, thus at one with all.
Through selfless action, he attains fulfillment.

– Lao Tzu

9

September

Why do what you will regret?
Why bring tears upon yourself?
Do only what you do not regret,
and fill yourself with joy.

– Buddha

10

September

When you accept yourself,
the whole world accepts you.

– Lao Tzu

11

September

Confused by thoughts, we experience duality in life.
Unencumbered by ideas, the enlightened see the one Reality.

– Huineng

12

September

Practice is this life, and realization is this life,
and this life is revealed right here and now.

– Taizan Maezumi

13
September

People usually fail when they are
on the verge of success. So give as much
care to the end as to the beginning.
Then there will be no failure.

– Lao Tzu

14
September

The miracle is not to walk on water.
The miracle is to walk on the green
Earth in the present moment,
to appreciate the peace and beauty
that are available now.

– Thich Nhat Hanh

15

September

The biggest help you can give a man
is to bring him inner freedom and peace.

– Taisen Deshimaru

16

September

The secret is within yourself.

– Huineng

17
September

In dwelling, live close to the ground.
In thinking, keep to the simple.

– Lao Tzu

18
September

Seek not happiness too greedily,
and be not fearful of happiness.

– Lao Tzu

19
September

Failure is the foundation
of success.

– Lao Tzu

20
September

Thousands of candles can be lighted
from a single candle, and the life
of the candle will not be shortened.
Happiness never decreases
by being shared.

– Buddha

21

September

The sage does not accumulate for himself.
The more he uses for others, the more he has for himself.
The more he gives to others, the more he possesses of his own.
The Way of Heaven is to benefit others and not to injure.

– Lao Tzu

22

September

When you see a good person, become like her/him.
When you see a bad person, reflect upon yourself.

– Confucius

23
September

Self–esteem can't be built in a day.
Everything takes time. If you make
courageous efforts day after day,
eventually you will gain confidence.

– Daisaku Ikeda

24
September
I never lost or fail, not yet conquered.
If I fall seven times, I get up eight.

– Bodhidharma

25
September

To talk little is natural.
High winds do not last all morning.
Heavy rain does not last all day.

– Lao Tzu

26
September

He who makes a show is not
enlightened. He who boasts achieves
nothing. He who brags will not endure.

– Lao Tzu

27
September

Knowing others is wisdom;
knowing the self is enlightenment.

– Lao Tzu

28
September

Man stands in his own shadow
and wonders why it's dark.

– Zen Proverb

29

September

When the mind stops moving,
it enters Nirvana.
Nirvana is an empty mind.

– Bodhidharma

30

September

The nature of one's own being where
apparently rages the struggle between the
finite and the infinite is to be grasped by a
higher faculty than the intellect. For Zen
says it is the latter that first made us raise the
question which it could not answer by itself.

– Daisetsu Teitarō Suzuki

1

October

I have just three things to teach:
simplicity, patience, compassion.
These three are your greatest treasures.
Simple in actions and in thoughts,
you return to the source of being.
Patient with both friends and enemies,
you accord with the way things are.
Compassionate toward yourself,
you reconcile all beings in the world.

– Lao Tzu

OCTOBER

2

October

Wisdom, compassion, and courage
are the three universally recognized
moral qualities of men.

– Confucius

3

October

What is meditation?
It is wisdom which is seeking
for wisdom.

– Shunryu Suzuki

4

October

Just live that life. It doesn't matter whether it is life or hell, life of the hungry ghost, life of the animal, it's okay; just live that life, see.

– Taizan Maezumi

5

October

Do not rely on following the degree of understanding that you have discovered, but simply think, "This is not enough."

– Tsunetomo Yamamoto

6
October

Our nature is the mind.
And the mind is our nature. [...]
They never stop invoking Buddhas
or worshipping Buddhas
and wondering where is the Buddha?
Don't indulge in such illusions.
Just know your mind.

– Bodhidharma

7
October

Generosity brings happiness at every
stage of its expression. We experience
joy in forming the intention to be
generous. We experience joy
in the actual act of giving something.
And we experience joy in remembering
the fact that we have given.

– Buddha

8

October

From a psychological point of view,
we can say that Zen liberates all the energies
stored in each of us, which are in ordinary
circumstances cramped and distorted.

– Daisetsu Teitarō Suzuki

9

October

To go back to yourself and dwell
in mindfulness is the best practice
in difficult moments.

– Thich Nhat Hanh

10

October

The superior man acts before
he speaks, and afterwards speaks
according to his action.

– Confucius

11

October

If you correct your mind, the rest
of your life will fall into place.

– Lao Tzu

12

October

Life is not a particular place
or destination. Life is a path.

– Thich Nhat Hanh

13

October

Wherever you go,
go with all your heart.

– Confucius

14

October

If we take care to regularly charge
our batteries, then we'll always be full
of energy and vitality. If we fail
to keep our batteries charged,
we won't have energy
when we need it most
and as a result may be defeated
by our environment.

– Daisaku Ikeda

15

October

Take care of things, and they will take
care of you.

– Shunryu Suzuki

16
October

No living thing should be killed,
not the smallest animal or insect,
for every life is sacred.

– Buddhist Quote

17
October

What you avoid suffering yourselves,
seek not to inflict upon others.

– Buddha

18

October

Look not to the faults of others,
nor to their omissions and commissions.
But rather look to your own acts,
to what you have done and left undone.

– Buddhist Quote

19

October

To hold, you must first
open your hand. Let go.

– Lao Tzu

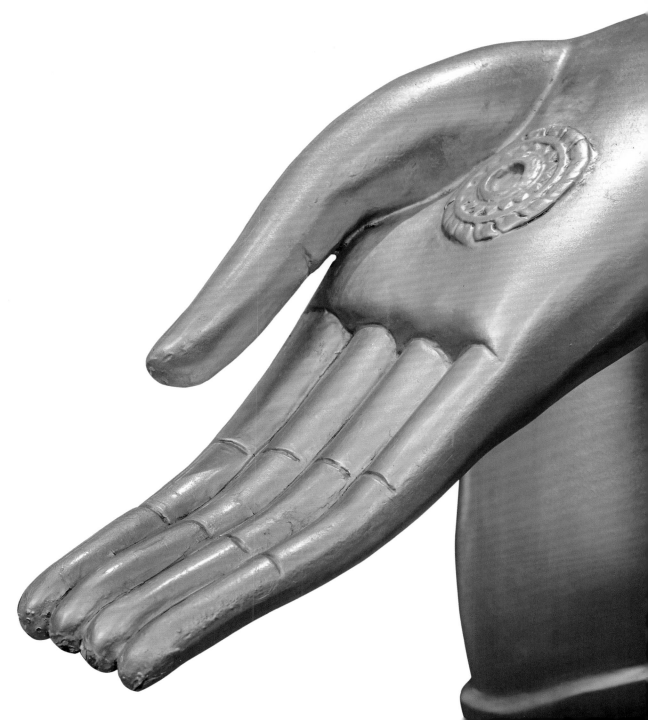

20

October

Better than sole sovereignty over the earth,
better than going to heaven,
better even than lordship over all the worlds
is the fruition of Stream–entry.

– Buddha

21

October

If you tighten the string of an instrument too much it will snap, and if you
leave it too slack it won't play. To Learn is to Change.
The path to enlightenment is in the Middle way.
It is the line between all opposite extremes.

– Buddha

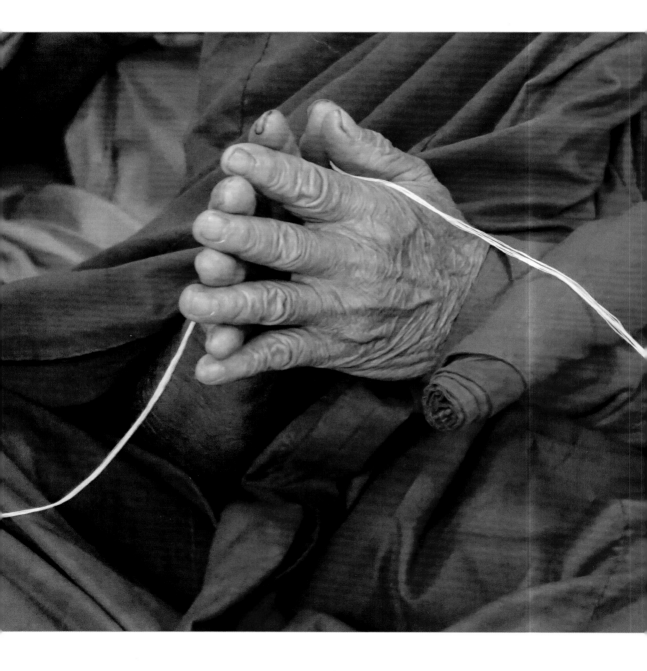

22
October

Good binders can dispense
with rope and cord, yet none can unloose
their hold.

– Lao Tzu

23
October

When you are content to be simply
yourself and don't compare or compete,
everybody will respect you.

– Lao Tzu

24
October

Over there are the roots of trees; over there,
empty dwellings. Practice jhana, monks.
Don't be heedless.

– Buddha

25
October

To refrain does not mean losing out; it shows
that you are using the gift of patience.

– Zen Proverb

26
October

Without going out of doors one may
know the whole world; without
looking out of the window, one may
see the Way of Heaven. Thus it is
that without moving you shall know;
without looking you shall see; without
doing you shall achieve.

– Lao Tzu

27
October

There is nothing permanent
except change.

– Buddha

28
October

The sage stays behind, thus he is ahead.
He is detached, thus at one with all.
Through selfless action,
he attains fulfillment.

– Lao Tzu

29
October

Walking is Zen, sitting is Zen;
whether we speak or are silent,
move or are still,
it is unperturbed.

– Wu-men

30

October

Manifest plainness, embrace simplicity,
reduce selfishness, have few desires.

– Lao Tzu

31

October

Keep your hands open, and all the sands of the desert can pass through them.
Close them, and all you can feel is a bit of grit.

– Taisen Deshimaru

1

November

Knowing others is wisdom;
Knowing the self is enlightenment.
Mastering others requires force, mastering the self needs strength.
He who knows he has enough is rich.
Perseverance is a sign of will power.
He who stays where he is endures.
To die but not to perish is to be eternally present.

– Lao Tzu

NOVEMBER

2
November

Forgetting oneself is opening oneself.

– Eihei Dōgen

3
November

The most important thing
is to find out what is
the most important thing.

– Shunryu Suzuki

4
November

If by setting one's heart right every
morning and evening, one is able to live as
though his body were already dead,
he gains freedom in the Way.

– Tsunetomo Yamamoto

5
November

As long as we remain within the confines
of the thinking mind, we can't experience
the state of non–thinking.
If we can't experience non–thinking,
we will not understand what our life
truly is. Please realize this for yourself!
Just sit.

– Taizan Maezumi

6

November

What we look at and can see is only
the outward form and color; what we
listen to and can hear is only names and
sounds. How can men think that form
and color, name and sound, are enough
to convey the real nature of anything!
Therefore: the wise do not speak and
those who do speak are not wise.

– Chuang Tzu

7

November

Time is a created thing.
To say "I don't have time", is like saying,
"I don't want to."

– Lao Tzu

8
November

The Tao begot one. One begot two.
Two begot three. And three begot the
ten thousand things. The ten thousand
things carry yin and embrace yang.
They achieve harmony by combining
these forces.

– Lao Tzu

9
November

He who wishes to secure the good
of others has already secured his own.

– Confucius

10
November

Even if you have mountains of jewels
and as many servants as there are grains
of sand along the Ganges, you see them
when your eyes are open. But what
about when your eyes are shut?

– Bodhidharma

11
November

Hatred does not cease by hatred,
but only by love; this is the eternal rule.
Suffering springs from the mind;
the path to the end of suffering
is in the mind.

– Buddha

12

November

Health is the greatest possession.
Contentment is the greatest treasure.
Confidence is the greatest friend.

– Lao Tzu

13

November

A man with outward courage
dares to die;
a man with inner courage
dares to live.

– Lao Tzu

14

November

Receive a guest with the same attitude
you have when alone. When alone,
maintain the same attitude you have
in receiving guests.

– *Soyen Shaku*

15

November

Silence is a friend only to the wise.

– *Zen Proverb*

16
November

A good soldier is not violent.
A good fighter is not angry.
A good winner is not vengeful.
A good employer is humble.

– Lao Tzu

17
November

In calmness there should be activity;
in activity there should be calmness.

– Shunryu Suzuki

18
November

Fame or self: Which matters more?
Self or wealth: Which is more precious?
Gain or loss: Which is more painful?
He who is attached to things
will suffer much.
He who saves will suffer heavy loss.
A contented man is never disappointed.

– Lao Tzu

19
November

Do unto others as you would have them
do unto you.

– Confucius

20

November

Do not think the knowledge you presently possess is changeless, absolute truth. Avoid being narrow–minded and bound to present views. Learn and practice non–attachment from views in order to be open to receive others' viewpoints. Truth is found in life and not merely in conceptual knowledge. Be ready to learn throughout your entire life and to observe reality in yourself and in the world at all times.

– Thich Nhat Hanh

21

November

When the mind reaches Nirvana, you don't see
Nirvana. Because the mind is Nirvana.
If you see Nirvana somewhere outside
the mind, you're deluding yourself.

– Bodhidharma

22

November

A finger points at the moon, but the moon
is not at the tip of the finger. Words points
at the truth, but the truth is not in words.

– Huineng

23

November

Your Six Canons are but the worn–out foot–
prints of ancient Sages. Foot–prints are made
by the shoe: they are not the shoe itself.

– Chuang Tzu

24
November

There is no greater sin than desire.
No greater curse than discontent,
No greater misfortune than wanting
something for oneself.

– Lao Tzu

25
November

If you have a reason,
you don't need to shout.

– Zen Proverb

26
November

Life is really simple,
but we insist on making it complicated.

– Confucius

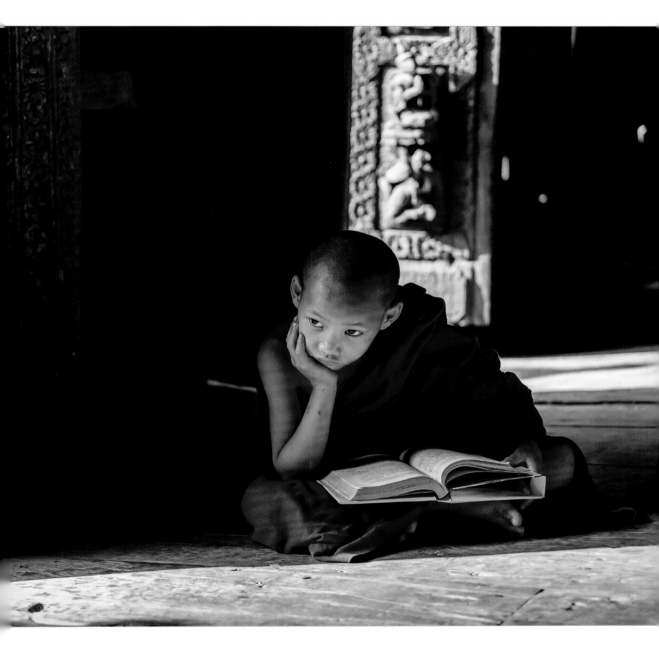

27
November

Is not life one as we live it, which we cut to pieces by recklessly applying the murderous knife of intellectual surgery?

– *Daisetsu Teitarō Suzuki*

28
November

Before you speak ask yourself if what you are going to say is true, is kind, is necessary, is helpful. If the answer is no, maybe what you are about to say should be left unsaid.

– *Buddha*

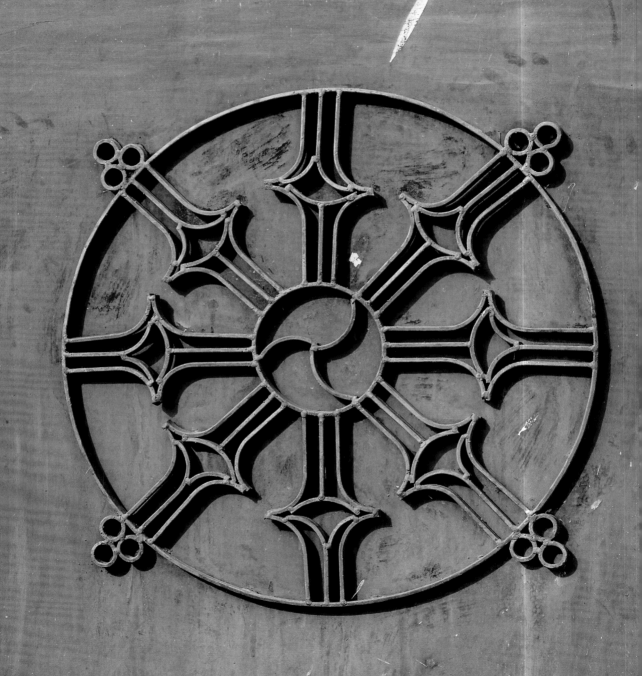

29

November

How much does he lack himself who must
have many things?

– Chuang Tzu

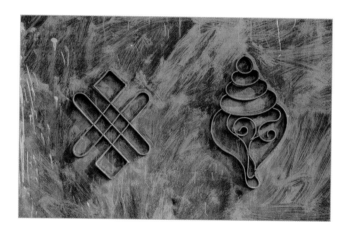

30

November

Treat every moment as your last.
It is not preparation for something else.

– Shunryu Suzuki

1

December

If there is to be peace in the world,
There must be peace in the nations.
If there is to be peace in the nations,
There must be peace in the cities.
If there is to be peace in the cities,
There must be peace between neighbors.
If there is to be peace between neighbors,
There must be peace in the home.
If there is to be peace in the home,
There must be peace in the heart.

– Lao Tzu

DECEMBER

2

December

To see form but not be corrupted by form or to hear sound
but not to be corrupted by sound is liberation.
Eyes that aren't attached to form are the gates of Zen.

– Bodhidharma

3

December

Have the fearless attitude of a hero
and the loving heart of a child.

– Soyen Shaku

4

December

What the caterpillar calls the end,
the rest of the world calls a butterfly.

– *Lao Tzu*

5

December

There is a being chaotically complete
in itself before heaven and earth
were born. Not knowing its name,
I call it "Tao."

– Lao Tzu

6

December

When affirmation and negation
came into being, Tao faded. After
Tao faded, then came one–sided
attachments.

– Chuang Tzu

7

December

Grace is not something that happens
sometimes and does not happen other
times; grace is always happening.
It is the very nature of existence. The
existence is grace–full. But sometimes
you get it and sometimes you miss it.

– Osho

8

December

If you don't lose your objectives
you can be long–lasting.

– Lao Tzu

9

December

What is more important:
succeeding or finding a sense
to your efforts to succeed?

– Shunryu Suzuki

10

December

If we keep thinking about all the
ways in which others have betrayed,
deceived, disappointed or angered us,
our heart will be forever full of hate.
Let us learn to let go, to be happy.

– Buddha

11

December

Passions arise in he who sees
the shortcomings of others and always
gets irritated, and he is far from
destroying them.

– Buddhist Quote

12

December

Pursue not the outer entanglements;
Dwell not in the inner void;
Be serene in the oneness of things;
And dualism vanishes by itself.

– Sengcan

13
December

Claim wealth and titles,
and disaster will follow.
Retire when the work is done.
This is the Way of heaven.

– Lao Tzu

14
December

Stay calm, don't be afraid; everything
will become clear. Do not worry, don't
panic; everything will fall into place.
This is the Way of the natural law.

– Lao Tzu

15
December

The greatest prayer
is patience.

– Buddha

16
December

It doesn't matter how slow you go,
as long as you do not stop.

– Confucius

17

December

Our own life is the instrument with which
we experiment with the truth.

– *Thich Nhat Hanh*

18

December

Your work is to discover your world and then
with all your heart give yourself to it.

– *Buddha*

19

December

A fool sees himself as another,
but a wise man sees others as himself.

– Eihei Dōgen

20

December

Pay no attention to the faults of others, things done or left undone by others.
Consider only what by oneself has done or left undone.

– Buddha

21
December

However many holy words you read,
however many you speak, what good
will they do you if you do not act
on upon them?

– Buddha

22
December

Prefer to be defeated in the presence
of the wise than to excel among fools.

– Eihei Dōgen

23

December

As long as you look for a Buddha
somewhere else, you'll never see that
your own mind is the Buddha.

– *Bodhidharma*

24
December

As one lamp serves to dispel years
of darkness, so one word of wisdom
destroys ten thousand years
of ignorance.

– Huineng

25
December

Time is not a line,
but a series of now-points.

– Taisen Deshimaru

26

December

The ego is the dark spot where the rays of the intellect fail to penetrate; it is the last hiding–lair of Ignorance, where the latter keeps itself from the light. When this lair is laid bare and turned inside out, Ignorance vanishes like frost in the sun.

– Daisetsu Teitarō Suzuki

27

December

We are what we think. All that we are arises with our thoughts. With our thoughts, we make the world.

– Buddha

28

December

To see the right and not to do it
is cowardice.

– Confucius

29

December

In this world of dreams, drifting off still
more; and once again speaking
and dreaming of dreams. Just let it be.

– Ryokan Taigu

30

December

In conflict, be fair and generous.
In governing, don't try to control.
In work, do what you enjoy.
In family life, be completely present.

– Lao Tzu

31

December

Life and death are of supreme
importance. Time swiftly passes by and
opportunity is lost. Each of us should
strive to awaken. Awaken! Take heed,
do not squander your life.

– Eihei Dōgen

LIST OF CONTRIBUTORS

B

Bodhidharma, 483-540 ca, Indian Buddhist monk (January 10, February 5, February 10, February 21, March 6, March 10, March 24, April 17, April 19, May 5, May 25, May 29, June 11, June 14, July 15, August 7, August 28, September 24, September 29, October 6, November 10, November 21, December 2, December 23)

Buddha, 566-486 B.C., Indian monk, philosopher, mystic and ascetic (January 2, January 1, January 4, January 12, January 19, January 26, January 27, February 4, February 13, April 1, April 4, April 5, April 7, April 8, April 14, April 24, April 26, May 1, May 3, May 15, May 28, May 30, June 10, June 23, July 11, July 16, July 18, July 24, August 22, August 27, September 9, September 20, October 7, October 17, October 20, October 21, October 24, October 27, November 11, November 28, December 10, December 15, December 18, December 20, December 21, December 27)

Buddhist Quote (January 5, January 11, January 23, March 28, May 14, October 16, October 18, December 11)

C

Chuang Tzu, 370-287 B.C., Chinese philosopher and mystic (February 16, March 20, May 6, June 7, June 21, July 1, July 26, August 10, November 6, November 23, November 29, December 6)

Confucius, 551-479 B.C., Chinese philosopher (February 7, February 19, February 20, March 2, March 21, March 25, April 6, June 4, June 9, June 27, July 29, August 4, September 2, September 22, October 2, October 10, October 13, November 9, November 19, November 26, December 16, December 28)

D

Daisaku Ikeda, 1928-, Japanese Buddhist master (February 9, July 19, August 23, September 23, October 14)

Daisetsu Teitarō Suzuki, 1870-1966, disseminator of Mahayana Buddhism and in particular of Zen Buddhism (January 7,

January 17, September 30,
October 8, November 27,
December 26)
Dengyo Daishi, 767-822,
Japanese Buddhist monk
(July 17)

E

Eihei Dōgen, 1200-1253,
Japanese Buddhist monk
(January 18, March 1,
March 29, April 29,
May 4, May 11, May 17,
May 18, June 3, June 19,
August 20, November 2,
December 19, December 22,
December 31)

H

Hakuin Ekaku, 1686-1769,
Japanese Buddhist monk
(January 22, February 27,
March 7, March 30,
April 10, May 2, July 21)

Hsuan Hua, 1918-1995,
Chinese Buddhist monk
(April 22, May 20)
Huangbo Xiyun, -849,
Chinese Buddhist master
(May 19, July 3, July 7,
July 30)
Huineng, 638-713, Chinese
Buddhist monk
(February 18, May 22,
June 16, July 28,
September 11, September 16,
November 22,
December 24)

I

Issa, Kobayashi, 1763-1828,
Japanese poet and
painter (March 4,
April 21)

K

Kōbō Daishi, 774-835
honorary title given to

Kukai, Japanese Buddhist
monk, founder of the
Shingon school of
Buddhism (June 24,
August 29)

L

Lao Tzu, 6th century B.C.,
Chinese philosopher
(January 3, January 13,
January 14, January 20,
January 29, February 3,
February 14, February 25,
February 22, February 23,
March 11, March 14,
March 17, March 18,
March 22, March 23,
March 26, March 27,
April 16, April 18,
April 20, April 23,
April 27, May 8, May 9,
May 10, May 16, May 21,
May 31, June 1, June 6,
June 8, June 12, June 15,
June 17, June 18, June 20,
June 25, June 30, July 10,

July 12, July 13, July 22, July 23, July 27, August 1, August 9, August 11, August 12, August 14, August 15, August 16, August 17, August 18, August 21, August 24, August 25, August 26, August 31, September 3, September 5, September 7, September 8, September 10, September 13, September 17, September 18, September 19, September 21, September 25, September 26, September 27, October 1, October 11, October 19, October 22, October 23, October 26, October 28, October 30, November 1, November 7, November 8, November 12, November 13, November 16, November 18, November 24, December 1, December 4, December 5, December 8, December 13, December 14, December 30)

Linji Yixuan, died in 866, Chinese Buddhist monk and founder of the Zen Rinzai school of Buddhism (May 27, September 6)

M

Matsuo Bashō, 1644-1694, Japanese poet (July 20)

O

Osho, 1931-1990, Indian mystic (August 6, December 7)

R

Ryokan Taigu, 1758-1831, Japanese Buddhist monk (March 5, August 3, August 19, December 29)

S

Sen no Rikyu, 1522-1591, Japanese Zen monk, (April 15)

Sengcan, -606, Third Chinese Patriarch of Chán (January 21, January 24, February 2, April 11, May 26, July 31, December 12)

Shenhui, 670-762, Chinese Buddhist monk (April 9, July 6)

Soyen Shaku, 1860-1919, Japanese Zen master (May 24, November 14, December 3)

Suzuki, Shunryu, 1904-1971, Japanese-born American Buddhist monk and teacher (March 31, April 28, June 26, August 2, October 3, October 15, November 3, November 17, November 30, December 9)

PHOTO CREDITS

Page 3: Worradirek Muksab/123RF
Page 4: Vittaya Aminsen/123RF

JANUARY

1, Byelikova_Oksana/iStockphoto; 2 and 3, Roberto Caucino/Shutterstock.com; 4 and 5, kieferpix/iStockphoto; 6 and 7, Tomaz Kunst/123RF; 8 and 9, guijunpen/123RF; 10 and 11, CHONNLAPOOM BANHARN/123RF; 12, Nirut Saelim/123RF; 13, szefei/123RF; 14 and 15, Leung Cho Pan/123RF; 16, 17 and 18, Klaus Hollitzer/iStockphoto; 19 and 20, Cai Liang/123RF; 21, Andreia Durante/Shutterstock.com; 22, eWilding/Shutterstock.com; 23 and 24, Kiwisoul/Shutterstock.com; 25 and 26, yamatao/iStockphoto; 27, Chalermphon Kumchai/123RF; 28, Chatchai Somwat/123RF; 29 and 30, unterwegs/Shutterstock.com; 31, ugurhan/iStockphoto.

FEBRUARY

1, Vyacheslav Cheremisin/123RF; 2, cowardlion/Shutterstock.com; 3, Chrislofotos/Shutterstock.com; 4 and 5, Bundit Jonwises/123RF; 6, Ping Han/123RF; 7, Yeung Kai Pak Patrick/123RF; 8 and 9, DanielPrudek/iStockphoto; 10, katyjay/123RF; 11 and 12, katyjay/123RF; 13, Kittikhun Prakrajang/123RF; 14, Mr. Bundit Chailaipanich/123RF; 15, Tawan Chaisom/123RF; 16, ugurhan/iStockphoto.com; 17 and 18, rweisswald/123RF; 19, msibbern/iStockphoto; 20, Claudiovidri/iStockphoto; 21 and 22, stefanocar75/iStockphoto; 23 and 24, Gita Kulinica/123RF; 25 and 26, Elegua/Shutterstock.com; 27, Direk Tomyim/123RF; 28 and 29, lakhesis/123RF.

MARCH

1, Graciela Rossi/123RF; 2, Braden Gunem/123RF; 3, Ping Han/123RF; 4 and 5, Sean Pavone/123RF; 6, 123RF; 7, Punnawit Suwattananum/123RF; 8, rweisswald/123RF; 9, southtownboy/iStockphoto; 10 and 11, Mikhail Priakhin/123RF; 12, Marina Pissarova/123RF; 13, FrankvandenBergh/iStockphoto; 14, 15 and 16, Leung Cho Pan/123RF; 17 and 18, lakhesis/123RF; 19, Nantarpat Surasingthothong/123RF; 20, Isriya Pratoomwong/123RF; 21 and 22, lkunl/iStockphoto; 23, 24 and 25, Phuong Nguyen Duy/123RF; 26

and 27, Chan Richie/123RF; 28, zanskar/iStockphoto; 29, zanskar/iStockphoto; 30 and 31, Sean Pavone Photo/iStockphoto.

APRIL

1, Elina Mylenka/123RF; 2, alantobey/iStockphoto; 3, Jakkarin Seema/123RF; 4, 5 and 6, yanukit/123RF; 7, 8 and 9, Andreas Metz/123RF; 10, 11 and 12, Rick Wang/Shutterstock.com; 13 and 14, ddukang/123RF; 15, Li Jiuming/123RF; 16, 17 and 18, Pavel Timofeev/123RF; 19 and 20, Phanupong Chuataew/123RF; 21, Teerapat Pattanasoponpong/123RF; 22, Nathapol Boonmangmee/123RF; 23, 24 and 25, photoroad/123RF; 26, Phuong D. Nguyen/Shutterstock.com; 27, Pikoso.kz/Shutterstock.com; 28, Yang Jun/123RF; 29 and 30, Nirut Saelim/123RF.

MAY

1, Ernst Christen/Shutterstock.com; 2 and 3, nvphoto/Shutterstock.com; 4, THANANIT SUNTIVIRIYANON/123RF; 5, dbajurin/123RF; 6 and 7, SantiPhotoSS/Shutterstock.com; 8 and 9, Vassiliy Kochetkov/123RF; 10 and 11, Checubus/Shutterstock.com; 12 and 13, R.M. Nunes/Shutterstock.com; 14 and 15 Thuansak Srilao/123RF; 16 and 17, Lorenzo Arcobasso/123RF;

18 and 19, shinnji/iStockphoto; 20, 21 and 22, Amnach Kinchokawat/123RF; 23, Jakgree Inkliang/123RF; 24, Yang Jun/123RF; 25, 26 and 27, Daniel Prudek/123RF; 28 and 29, Daniel Prudek/123RF; 30, Medtech THAI STUDIO LAB 249/ Shutterstock.com; 31, Chatree.I/Shutterstock.com.

JUNE

1, Petr Goskov/123RF; 2, Nikolay Mossolaynen/123RF; 3 and 4, Ping Han/123RF; 5, Thomas Dutour/123RF; 6, Thomas Dutour/123RF; 7, Trinette Monkel/123RF; 8, Trinette Monkel/123RF; 9 and 10, Theerawat Payakyut/123RF; 11 and 12, alsimonov/123RF; 13 and 14, Sarayuth Nutteepratoom/123RF; 15 and 16, saiko3p/123RF; 17 and 18, RoelBeurskens/iStockphoto; 19 and 20, Miroslav Liska/123RF; 21 and 22, subinpumsom/iStockphoto; 23 and 24, Vectortone/Shutterstock.com; 25, Jan Gerrit Siesling/123RF; 26, Neven Milinkovic/123RF; 27 and 28, naihei/iStockphoto; 29, coward_lion/iStockphoto; 30, coward_lion/iStockphoto

JULY

1, zzvet/123RF; 2, blanscape/123RF; 3, Matteo Ercole/123RF; 4, deaphen/123RF; 5, deaphen/

123RF; 6, Hung_Chung_Chih/iStockphoto; 7, DanielPrudek/iStockphoto; 8 and 9, 69Studio/Shutterstock.com; 10 and 11, Iryna Rasko/123RF; 12, stockphoto mania/Shutterstock.com; 13, noomcm/Shutterstock.com; 14 and 15, Martibn Molcan/123RF; 16 and 17, Surachet99/iStockphoto; 18 and 19, yurok/123RF; 20, hadynyah/iStockphoto; 21, Smitt/iStockphoto; 22 and 23, Yang Jun/123RF; 24 and 25, Aliaksandr Mazurkevich/123RF; 26, Sergey Trifonov/123RF; 27, Pawel Opaska/123RF; 28, Cai Liang/123RF; 29, Pakin Songmor/123RF; 30 and 31, Pan Demin/123RF.

AUGUST

1, Ugurhan Betin/iStockphoto; 2 and 3, Wang Xiaomin/123RF; 4, Law Alan/123RF; 5, Law Alan/123RF; 6 and 7, afe207/123RF; 8, Nattee Chalermtiragool/123RF; 9, Stefano Tronci/123RF; 10, Kittikhun Prakrajang/123RF; 11, Apirati Pumruangnam/123RF; 12 and 13, Sean Pavone/123RF; 14, 15 and 16, mesamong/123RF; 17, Keng Po Leung/123RF; 18, Jamie Farrant/123RF; 19 and 20, alsimonov/123RF; 21 and 22, Anton Yankovyi/123RF; 23, Krzysztof StĐpieĐ/123RF; 24, fischel/123RF; 25 and 26, FooTToo/iStockphoto; 27 and 28, Tanakom Pussawong/Shutterstock.

com; 29, Zoltan Szabo Photography/Shutterstock.com; 30, Zoltan Szabo Photography/Shutterstock.com; 31, pat138241/123RF.

SEPTEMBER

1, wklzzz/123RF; 2 and 3, Tanee Sawasdee/Shutterstock.com; 4 and 5, ppart/Shutterstock.com; 6, Apple_Foto/Shutterstock.com; 7 and 8, Sarayut Mathavetchathum/123RF; 9 and 10, Tawan Chaisom/123RF; 11 and 12, briancweed/iStockphoto; 13 and 14, Daniel Prudek/123RF; 15, CHIH HSIEN HANG/123RF; 16, CHIH HSIEN HANG/123RF; 17, R.M. Nunes/Shutterstock.com; 18, Jenny Rainbow/Shutterstock.com; 19 and 20, Taiwan Chaisom/123RF; 21, Zzvet/iStockphoto; 22, Zzvet/iStockphoto; 23 and 24, NATALYA LIKHASCHENKO/123RF; 25 and 26, Zephyr18/iStockphoto; 27, SANCHAI LOONGROONG/123RF; 28, rawpixel/123RF; 29 and 30, Tul Chalothonrangsee/123RF.

OCTOBER

1, photoroad/123RF; 2 and 3, Blanscape/Shutterstock.com; 4, dinozzaver/123RF; 5, dinozzaver/123RF; 6 and 7 Kittiphat Inthonprasit/123RF; 8 and 9, Dmitry Islentyev/123RF; 10, lovelyday12/iStockphoto; 11, Mlenny/iStockphoto; 12 and 13, hadynyah/iStockphoto; 14 and 15, Peera Sathawirawong/123RF; 16, autsawin uttisin/Shutterstock.com; 17, autsawin uttisin/Shutterstock.com; 18 and 19, Anuwat Ratsamerat/123RF; 20, guenterguni/iStockphoto; 21, guenterguni/iStockphoto; 22, Tanantornanutra/iStockphoto; 23, Kobchai Matasurawit/123RF; 24, wanderluster/iStockphoto; 25, sergwsq/iStockphoto; 26 and 27, Tomaz Kunst/123RF; 28 and 29, Anucha Yossuwan/123RF; 30, aluxum/iStockphoto; 31, amadeustx/123RF.

NOVEMBER

1, R.M. Nunes/Shutterstock.com; 2, Nila Newsom/123RF; 3, Nila Newsom/123RF; 4 and 5, Pongmanat Tasiri/123RF; 6 and 7, Byelikova_Oksana/iStockphoto; 8 and 9, Luciano Mortula/123RF; 10 and 11, saiko3p/123RF; 12 and 13, Zoltan Szabo Photography/Shutterstock.com; 14 and 15, THANANIT SUNTIVIRIYANON/123RF; 16 and 17, SUMITH NUNKHAM/Shutterstock.com; 18 and 19, Daniel Prudek/123RF; 20, Von Allmen Helena/123RF; 21, 22 and 23, Cai Liang/123RF; 24, shirophoto/iAStockphoto; 25, Kanyarat Wongtip/123RF; 26, Tawan Chaison/123RF; 27 and 28, Zhao jian kang/Shutterstock.com; 29, Phuong Nguyen Duy/123RF; 30, Phuong Nguyen Duy/123RF.

DECEMBER

1, Nudda Chollamark/123RF; 2, FRANCISCO GONZALES SANCHEZ/123RF; 3, FRANCISCO GONZALES SANCHEZ/123RF; 4, Li Jiuming/123RF; 5 and 6, foodandmore/123RF; 7 and 8, Nila Newsom/123RF; 9 and 10, Tropical studio/Shutterstock.com; 11 and 12, Pakin Songmor/123RF; 13 and 14, Vaclav Apl/123RF; 15 and 16, Ping Han/123RF; 17, szefei/123RF; 18, szefei/123RF; 19, Pravich Vutthisombut/123RF; 20, Montri Pramchuen/123RF; 21 and 22, mail11/Shutterstock.com; 23, Chairat Rattana/123RF; 24 and 25, Marina Pissarova/123RF; 26, szefei/123RF; 27, Nirut Saelim/123RF; 28 and 29, Vaclav Apl/123RF; 30 and 31, Thana Thanadechakul/Shutterstock.com.

COVER: Tawan Chaisom/123RF
BACK COVER, top from the left: Apple_Foto/Shutterstock.com; Byelikova_Oksana/iStockphoto, Dmitry Islentyev/123RF

Project Editor
Valeria Manferto De Fabianis

Editorial assistant
Laura Accomazzo

Graphic layout
Valentina Giammarinaro

WHITE STAR PUBLISHERS

WS White Star Publishers® is a registered trademark
property of White Star s.r.l.

© 2017 White Star s.r.l.
Piazzale Luigi Cadorna, 6 - 20123 Milan, Italy
www.whitestar.it

Translation: and Editing: TperTradurre s.r.l.

ISBN 978-88-544-1182-1
1 2 3 4 5 6   21 20 19 18 17

Printed in China